BARKING TO SOUTHEND

Dr. Edwin Course

Series editor Vic Mitchell

 Middleton Press

*Cover picture: The 1.40pm (Sundays only) from Shoeburyness to Fenchurch Street runs into Upminster on 22nd August 1926. The locomotive, LMSR no. 2176, had been built for the LTSR in 1909 by Robert Stephenson & Sons as no. 76 **Rippleside** and was not withdrawn until 1951.*

Published April 2002
First reprint January 2005

ISBN 1 901706 80 X

© Middleton Press, 2002

Design   Deborah Esher
Typesetting   Barbara Mitchell

Published by
          Middleton Press
          Easebourne Lane
          Midhurst, West Sussex
          GU29 9AZ
Tel: 01730 813169
Fax: 01730 812601
Email: info@middletonpress.co.uk
www.middletonpress.co.uk

Printed & bound by Biddles Ltd, Kings Lynn

CONTENTS

ACKNOWLEDGEMENTS

I would like to express my thanks to the photographers for the assistance received and also to my wife Catherine Course for typing the text. I am also grateful to Godfrey Croughton, for supplying ticket copies, and to Dave Brennand for help with the maps.

I. The route diagram from the early 20th century has had a few of the later stations added. (M.Harris)

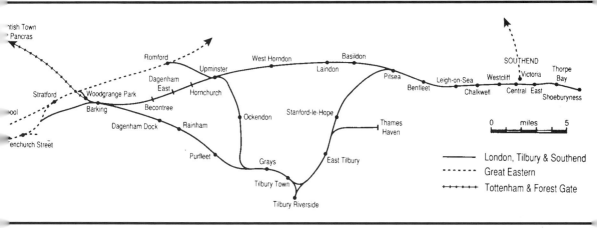

GEOGRAPHICAL SETTING

The line between Barking and Pitsea was built across the relatively flat farmland of South Essex. There were no towns to be served although a divergence from a straight line was made to reach the villages of Hornchurch and Upminster. The only physical feature to influence the route was the high ground of the Langdon Hills, which reach a height of 386 feet. This gave rise to about 1½ miles of line with a gradient of 1 in 110. Apart from road bridges, there were minor structures over the Rivers Beam and Ingrebourne, a considerable cutting at Upminster, and a series of banks and cuttings in the Laindon area. These were constructed through clay and were prone to instability.

At Pitsea, the new cut-off line joined the original line from Tilbury to Southend. Beyond this junction, the original line followed the foot of the hills across the marshland, rising to clear a spur of higher ground at Benfleet. It then crossed the marshes to Leigh-on-Sea from which it was planned to follow the shore line to a terminal near Southend Pier. However, a railway along the top of the beach, in Dawlish style, aroused so much opposition that it was diverted inland, climbing up from the shore at 1 in 94 to a terminal rather less than half a mile north of the Pier. The line from here was extended over farmland to the military base at Shoeburyness.

By 2001 much of the country traversed had been built upon. There were no longer any breaks in the spread of housing as far as Upminster, and very few between Leigh-on-Sea and Shoeburyness. Thus the present day passenger between Barking and Shoeburyness sees little open country.

All the maps are to the scale of 25ins to 1 mile, unless otherwise shown.

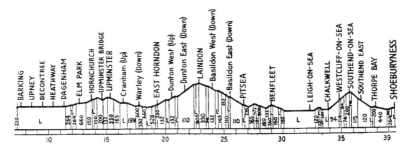

II. Gradient profile, with mileage from Fenchurch Street.

HISTORICAL BACKGROUND

As its coat of arms shows, the London, Tilbury & Southend Railway served Tilbury (represented by Tilbury Fort) also London, Kent and Essex. In its early days a better title would have been the London, Gravesend and Southend Railway as Tilbury was no more than a transfer point for steamers to Gravesend and other places reached by water. However, it was not the intention to leave the Southend traffic to steamers. The powers of the 1852 Act, under which the original line was constructed, covered a branch from the Eastern Counties Railway at Forest Gate to Tilbury, with an extension from there to Southend. Tilbury was reached on 13th April 1854, Leigh on 1st July 1855 and Southend on 1st March 1856. It was promoted jointly by the Eastern Counties and the London & Blackwall Railways and competed with the highly successful paddle steamers and with the South Eastern Railway's line to Gravesend. With backing from three sources - the Eastern Counties, the London & Blackwall and independent shareholders - it was not a conventional joint line. To add to the complexity, until 1875 the line was leased to the contractors, Peto, Brassey & Betts, who provided the services with rolling stock hired from the Eastern Counties Railway. (This became the Great Eastern Railway in 1862). However, the independent shareholders, who included a number of influential individuals, demonstrated their wish to influence the running of the line and finally the London, Tilbury & Southend became independent. When in 1875, the lease to Peto, Brassey & Betts ended, the

Board took over operations with considerable success.

Perhaps more than was usual, developments were initiated by the LTSR General Manager. He was Arthur Lewis Stride, appointed in 1875 and retiring as chairman when the company was taken over by the Midland Railway in 1912.

To give a more direct line to Southend, a cut-off was built between Barking and Pitsea. It was opened in stages: Barking to Upminster on 1st May 1885, on to East (now West) Horndon on 1st May 1886 and the section to Pitsea finally completing the route on 1st June 1888. Impetus to build the new cut-off line owed something to the decision of the Great Eastern Railway to construct a competing route to Southend, which was opened in 1889. With the cut-off, the distance from Fenchurch Street to Southend was 36 miles compared to Liverpool Street to Southend, at 41 miles. The line was extended from Southend to Shoeburyness on 1st February 1884. The route from Tilbury to Romford through Upminster was opened in 1893.

With the passage of time, the cut-off line acquired its own intermediate traffic. In LTS days this was mainly high class residential traffic from Hornchurch and Upminster. Although the Midland Railway take-over came in 1912, they were unable to undertake any major development before the outbreak of war in 1914. In 1923, the MR became part of the London, Midland & Scottish Railway, which was responsible for the changes of the 1930s. It introduced a new class

LTSR Coat of Arms.

of locomotive, adapted to suit the lines and provided new coaches. In 1932 an additional two tracks were added between Barking and Upminster, available for District line electric trains. These services were transferred to London Transport in 1933. New stations were added at Upney, Heathway, Elm Park and Upminster Bridge and the existing stations at Dagenham, Gale Street, Hornchurch and Upminster were rebuilt. The LTS had built two new stations in the Southend area at Westcliff and Thorpe Bay and the LMS added another two, at Chalkwell and Southend East. It provided a new building on a new site at Leigh-on-Sea. At the outbreak of war in 1939, although still steam operated, the route was served by frequent, punctual passenger services.

With the return of peace in 1945, recovery was slow and following nationalisation in 1948 British Railways inherited a somewhat run-down line. In 1949, in a way, a delayed Great Eastern take over materialised, when the route was transferred from the London Midland to the Eastern Region. However, all was to improve with the advent of electrification on 6th November 1961, although then only partial. The traditional traffic control with semaphore signals, and the steam hauled trains finally disappeared in June 1962.

After this great improvement, there were only minor changes for some years. In 1970 the stations and double track electric line between Barking and Upminster were transferred to London Transport and became independent from the BR tracks. The Southend line trains called only at Barking and Upminster subsequently and the platforms at intermediate stations fell into disuse, but in 1974 a station was opened for Basildon New Town. By the late 1980s there was a degree of rundown and the Press bestowed the name "Misery Line" on the route to Southend. Plans for a revival had been formulated before the line was privatised on 26th May 1996 for a 15-year term. Traffic control was concentrated on one centre, at Upminster, and new trains were to be provided. At the time of writing in 2001, improved signalling has materialised and new trains are being introduced. The private operators abandoned their initial title of LTS Rail and in 2000 introduced the initials c2c, to suggest "city to the sea". The general reaction to this unindexable howler is unprintable, as many other routes serve this function and LTS has been meaningful for almost 150 years.

PASSENGER SERVICES

The London, Tilbury and Southend Railway earned a significant part of its revenue from freight, but this originated mainly on the Tilbury to Barking section. On the Southend direct line, passenger revenue was dominant and has always remained so. Despite competition from the Great Eastern route and earlier from the paddle steamers, the route has always carried most of the Southend traffic. By 1936 it was estimated that on a Bank Holiday Monday, the line carried between 60,000 and 70,000 passengers to Southend and back; this would have required trains at something like five minute intervals. Whilst most trains ran from Fenchurch Street there were also excursions from the Midland line and the London & North Western line. The importance for revenue depended on the large numbers; for many years the standard Day Return Fare was 2/6d. Apart from the operating problems imposed by the day excursion traffic, it required the maintenance of a considerable amount of old coaching stock and was vulnerable to weather conditions.

Whilst the traditional railway felt bound to carry all traffic offered, there is no doubt that both staff and management preferred the season ticket holders. They were better behaved and travelled regularly each day. Particularly after the opening of the direct line to Southend in 1888, the number of Southend season ticket holders increased. In that year the most prestigious train left at 9.10am and reached Fenchurch Street at 10.00am. In 1938 the 9.00am made a call at Westcliff and arrived at the City terminal at 9.52am. In 1956 the best time was 1 hour 10 minutes and in 2001, with electric traction, the 09.05hrs took 50 minutes but with five stops.

The 1938 LMS timetable commended London's Nearest Seaside Resorts: Leigh, Chalkwell, Westcliff and Southend-on-Sea; under the hour from London (Fenchurch Street).The increasing importance of stations other than Southend Central was recognised by 'skipping'. For instance, in the morning a train started from Thorpe Bay at 8.45 and ran through Southend East and Southend Central, picking up at Westcliff, Chalkwell and Leigh.

After the impact of the Second World War the route suffered a bad period. In 1956 the best train was taking 1 hour 10 minutes and the average time for the 36 miles was 1 hour 25 minutes. Far from providing a shorter time than the Brighton line, the journey to Southend now took longer. The Southend-on-Sea Travellers Association quoted an assessment that "Travelling between Fenchurch Street and Southend has become a national joke". With electrification in 1962 came relief but by the 1990s there was a new phase of deterioration. In 1992 the Independent Magazine carried an illustrated article entitled "The Misery Line". In 2001, with new trains and a new signalling system, things improved. For the first time since 1912 the route has independent management and there is hope of a return to LTS standards of reliability.

In 2001, during the off-peak period, there were four trains an hour at fixed intervals, the fast trains taking 52 minutes with 8 stops and the slower taking 1 hour 8 minutes with 13 stops. At the London end, since 2000, connections to other parts of London have been improved by calls at West Ham. The general picture is one of more trains running with more stops.

Up weekday trains in September in 1885, when Upminster was a rural terminus.

Part of the up morning train service on weekdays in July 1914.

BARKING

III.   The station became a junction in 1858 when the direct line from Bow reached it, avoiding Stratford. However, some trains continued to run to the Tilbury line from Liverpool Street. In 1894 the Tottenham & Forest Gate Railway was opened, joining the original line at Forest Gate and adding traffic from St. Pancras and the Midland lines to the LTS at Barking. In 1888 the direct line to Southend via Upminster was completed, diverging immediately east of Barking. In addition to being a junction point, Barking also became a terminal for suburban services; extra platforms were added in 1889. From 1908 Barking became the outer terminal for the District line electric trains. The station was rebuilt with four island platforms, the level crossing was replaced by an overbridge and new buildings constructed on the bridge. When the District train service was extended to Upminster in 1932, some alterations were made in the tracks but there were no major changes until the electrification of the main lines was completed in 1962. The junctions, both to the east and to the west, were rebuilt with flyovers and diveunders to avoid conflicting movements. New buildings were provided at street level and the utilisation of the platforms was altered. The map is from 1939.

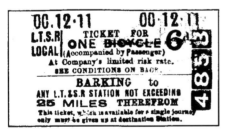

Other views of this station, can be found in
Fenchurch Street to Barking
(Middleton Press)

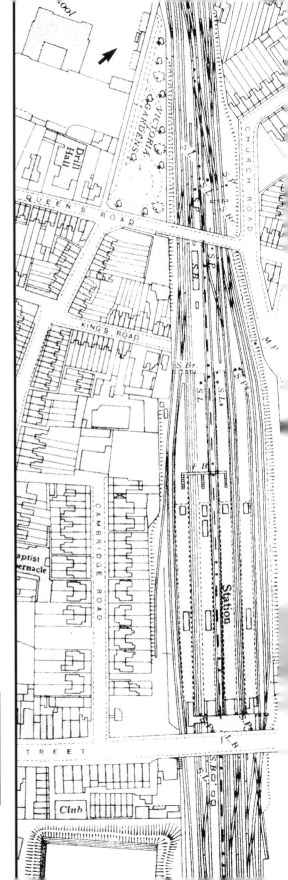

1.   This view was taken from the footbridge which spanned the four island platforms in the steam period. A down excursion train from the St. Pancras line was passing platform 6 on 14th September 1957, en route for Southend. The corridor connection indicates the use of Midland line stock. The buildings of 1908 are in use on the platforms and at street level. (H.C.Casserley)

2.   Another view from the bridge, taken on 14th October 1957, shows all four island platforms still gas lit, the end of the West Signal Box and Queens Road overbridge. The guards compartment and the luggage section of the leading former LMS coach are visible. No. 42533 was one of the 36 2-6-4 3-cylinder tank engines built at Derby in 1934. The use of 3 cylinders was to persuade the LNER Civil Engineer to permit them to operate over the viaduct into Fenchurch Street, with reduced hammerblow. The train was the 1.15pm from Shoeburyness to Fenchurch Street. West Signal Box controlled both BR and LT trains with a mixture of semaphores and colour light signals. (F.Church)

3.   The third view was taken from platform 3 on 5th October 1957 and shows no. 42521, another of the 2-6-4 T Derby built locomotives of 1934, taking water. Normally the 2,000 gallon capacity of the side tanks was sufficient to avoid the need for taking water en route, but this was a Southend to St. Pancras train. The level of water was ascertained visually and this is what the fireman is doing. This view also shows semaphore signals and a fog repeater with colour lights. (F.Church)

4.   This picture is from the East Signal Box and shows a train leaving for Southend in about 1950. No. 2532, another of the batch built at Derby in 1934, hauls a train of ex-Midland compartment coaches. There were no set rules about the direction in which locomotives faced, and although in this case it was running with the smokebox leading, this was not invariable. The background includes the 1908 street level buildings, with a trolleybus passing, a typical 1930s super cinema and part of the goods yard with a mechanical horse. (H.C.Doyle)

5.   When this view was taken from the East Street bridge on 24 August 1957, some of the work on rebuilding the two junctions had begun. It shows the original line of 1854 going straight ahead for Tilbury and the Southend direct route diverging to the left with the East Signal Box in the fork. A typical train, with a Stanier 2-6-4 T locomotive, is approaching and a London Transport train departs on the left. The terraced housing characteristic of Barking, owes much to the presence of the railway. (A.A.Jackson)

6.   The footbridge at the end of Erkenwald Road, which appears in the previous photograph, provided the viewpoint for this shot on 23rd March 1957. No. 90653, a former WD 2-10-0, is leaving the goods yard, which closed on 1st April of that year. (R.C.Riley)

7.   This was the view from the same footbridge on 3rd April 1986. The goods yard has been replaced by London Transport sidings and the LT train is descending to the diveunder east of Barking. (E.Course)

8.   The final view of Barking was taken from platform 5 on 19th September 1990 and shows the type of train associated with the first phase of electrification; that is the early 1960s until the late 1990s. It shows Set 302 228 running in on a train for Pitsea. (M.Turvey)

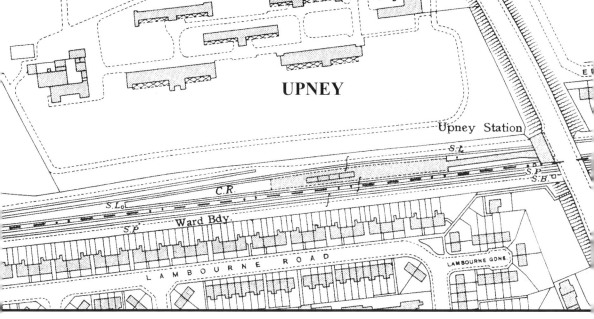

UPNEY

IV.   The part of the direct line to Southend, between Barking and Upminster, changed in character in 1932. Two electrified tracks were added for use by District line electric trains and are shown on the north side of this 1939 map, along with Barking's longest siding. A number of new stations were opened by the LMS and existing stations adapted as necessary. In 1970, the transfer of tracks and stations to London Transport was completed and they became isolated from the Southend line. The new developments reflected the mushroom growth of Becontree and Dagenham, and a little later of Hornchurch and Upminster, between the wars. Four new stations were opened and the existing four were rebuilt. Although the work was done by the LMS all four of the new stations were served by London Transport only. The first of these was Upney where the following three views were taken on 12th September 1980.

9.   The first shows the view from the single island platform looking towards Barking, as a train proceeds towards Southend on the down main line. The length of LT trains was limited by the length of platforms on the underground sections, so the end of the Upney platform was disused. BR built 112 4-car sets of this type at Doncaster for the Southend services. Each had 344 second class seats and 19 firsts. (A.A.Jackson)

10.   The second view shows a westbound LT train about to pick up waiting pasengers. Apart from the LT nameboards, little has changed since the days of LMS ownership in the 1930s. (A.A.Jackson)

11.   The third view taken from the roadway shows a more cautious approach to contemporary style than that to be found on LT buildings of similar date. In LMS days, the canopy was marked with the initials 'LMS' and the name of the station. Most passengers were expected to arrive on foot and there is no layby for road vehicles. (A.A.Jackson)

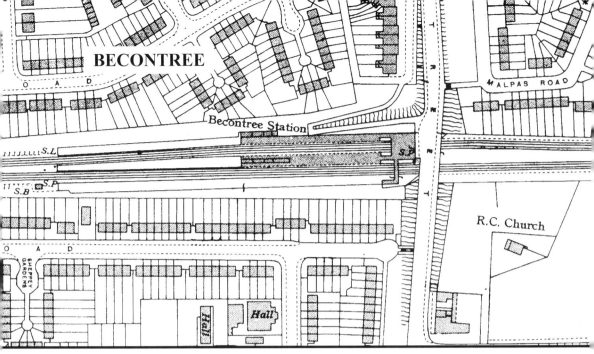

BECONTREE

Becontree Station

R.C. Church

V.   The LMS had opened a halt here called 'Gale Street' on 28th June 1926. New tracks were added in 1932 and the halt was replaced by a new station called 'Becontree' on 18th July 1932, shown on this 1938 map. Like the other new stations it catered for passengers only and had the booking office at road level. The widening of the lines was accompanied by some new signalling arrangements. Gale Street Intermediate Box was replaced by a new Intermediate Box called 'Becontree'.

12.   The photograph shows the small cabin and traditional chaired rails with wooden sleepers. The up train seen on 30th November 1957 is hauled by no. 42533, a 3 cylinder 2-6-4 T, another of the batch built at Derby in 1934. (F.Church)

13.   The second view, taken on 12th September 1980 from the eastbound platform, shows the station as transferred to London Transport in 1970. The main line platforms had been disused since 1962 and the platform buildings removed. (A.A.Jackson)

DAGENHAM HEATHWAY

14.   This station was virtually a repeat of Upney, built to serve the massive concentration of London County Council housing. The view of 12th September 1980, shows the single island platform with access from a roadover bridge. The train on the main line is en route to Southend. (A.A.Jackson)

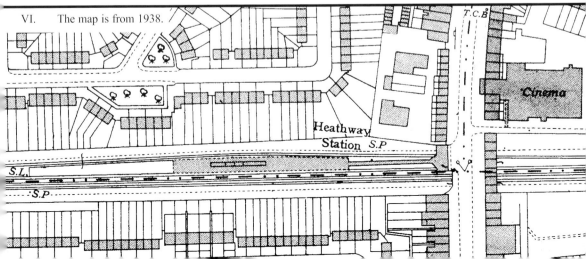

VI.   The map is from 1938.

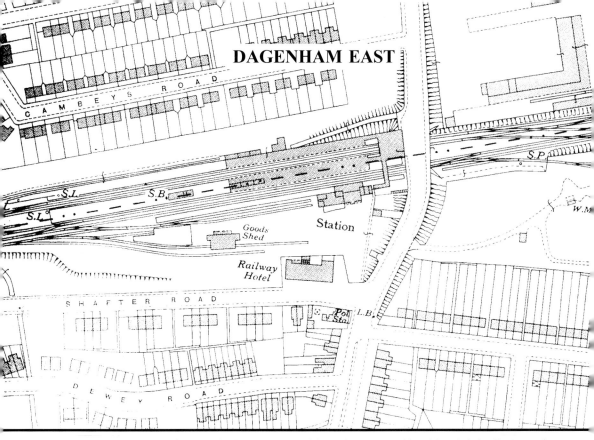

DAGENHAM EAST

VII.   This was one of the original country wayside stations opened in 1885. Originally Dagenham, it was renamed Dagenham East on 1st May 1949. BR trains ceased to call in 1961 and it was closed to goods traffic on 6th May 1968. Top right is the convergence of two long sidings serving a chemical works. They are seen on the 1939 edition.

15.   This shows the station virtually as built, complete with booking office, station masters house and goods shed. The telegraph lines are a prominent feature and an oil lamp is visible. (Commercial postcard)

16.   The second view was taken on 5th October 1957. The LT tracks had been constructed on the north side leaving the original buildings and goods shed virtually untouched. Also in the view are the traditional signal box, the gas lights and the 11¼ Mile Post (distance from Fenchurch Street). A terminal bay was added on the eastbound side in 1935 for the reversal of LT trains not running through to Upminster. (F.Church)

17.   The bay was occupied on 12th September 1980. The destination shows 'Richmond', indicating the way in which people on these former LTSR stations could make through cross London journeys. The electric train carries an oil tail lamp, still then obligatory. (A.A.Jackson)

18.   The fourth view also dated 12th September 1980 shows the 1932 buildings which replaced those of 1885. These were taken over by LT in 1970, but there have been only minor changes subsequently. The covered footbridge to the left carried passengers to the main line platforms when they were in use. (A.A.Jackson)

VIII.   Elm Park resembled Upney and Dagenham Heathway, but was linked to private development rather than council housing. It was opened three years later on 13th May 1935. The 1938 survey is scaled at 6ins to 1 mile and shows the limited building at that time.

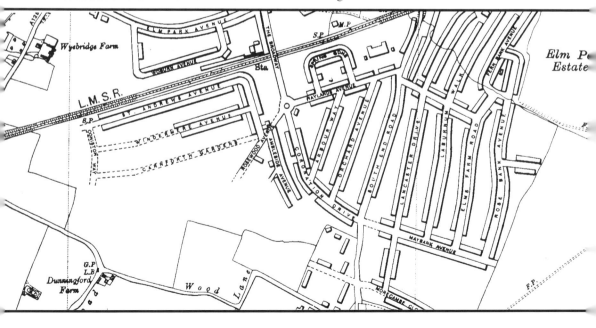

ELM PARK

19.　　A shot taken on 12th September 1980 shows the entrance building. Writing about this in his book, *London, Tilbury and Southend Album,* George Dow says "Not the entrance to an amusement arcade but to Elm Park station, it is the vulgar climax of a passing fashion which the LMS, with the noble architectural traditions of the Midland as a heritage, should have been ashamed to adopt". The typical terrace of 1930s shops, with living accommodation over, belongs to the same period. (A.A.Jackson)

20.　　The second view taken at the same time shows the island platform with its ramp, rather than steps, leading to road level. (A.A.Jackson)

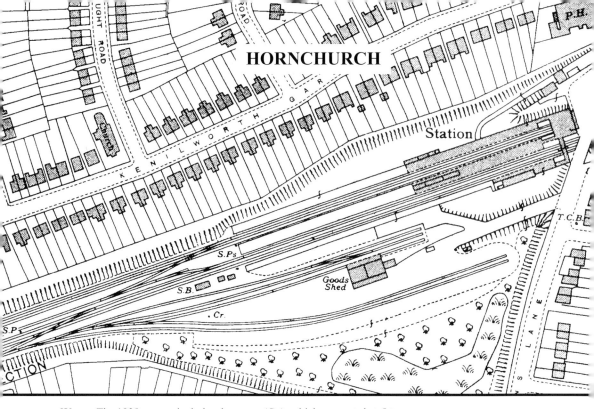

HORNCHURCH

Station

IX. The 1939 survey includes the crane (Cr.), which was rated at 5 tons.

21. Of the two LTS stations of 1885 between Barking and Upminster, Hornchurch was the most important. It was still a wayside station in the early 1910s, serving a small country town in a rural area. The station masters house and the booking hall were at road level, but not built on the bridge over the railway. The viewpoint from the up platform shows the station buildings and the ample goods shed, prior to quadrupling. Details include the gas lamps, the platform seats and the porters trolley. (Loco Publishing /Real Photographs)

22.   This view is dated 14 August 1909 and is taken from the bank at the London end of the station. The train for Fenchurch Street consists of a luggage van and LTS 4-wheel coaches. The locomotive was recorded as no. 60 *Highgate Road* built by Sharp, Stewart in 1900 and finally withdrawn in 1956. Until the Second World War the practice of locomotives on passenger trains carrying a destination board was followed. On this train the board is marked 'Fenchurch'. Above it is a board marked 'LTSR' for the information of GE signalmen, and below, a white disc with a red cross indicating the route to be followed. Also showing is the original signal box of 1885 (replaced in 1930) and a tall signal post with co-acting arms for the assistance of drivers approaching from beyond the overbridge. (K.Nunn/LCGB)

23.   This photograph from 30th November 1957 was taken from the former up platform which became the centre island platform. The goods shed is off the picture to the right but additional tracks and new buildings appear on the left. (F.Church)

24.   This 12th September 1980 view shows the former LTS platforms, closed in 1961, and the goods shed closed to rail traffic in 1981. Subsequently the site of the goods depot was sold. (A.A.Jackson)

25.   The station forecourt was also recorded on 12th September 1980. It was re-designed in 1932 with the original LTS buildings replaced by a modern entrance. In contrast to the other stations, Hornchurch has adequate space for road vehicles including buses. (A.A.Jackson)

UPMINSTER BRIDGE

26.   The photograph is from 12th September 1980 and was taken from the overbridge on the London side of the station. A class 302 bound for Fenchurch Street appears on the right. Upminster Bridge was opened on 17th December 1934 to serve middle class housing development. Like the other new stations, it consisted of an island platform, but this was above rather than below road level. The entrance failed to please George Dow who particularly disliked two unusual lampposts which he described as "Odeonesque, a very kind way of putting it". However, despite his adverse comment they were still in place at least until 1980. (A.A.Jackson)

<table>
<tr><td>L.M.&S.R. For
conditions see Back
THIRD CLASS
SINGLE</td><td>L.M.&S.R. For
conditions see Back
THIRD CLASS
SINGLE</td></tr>
<tr><td>Heathway
Heathway</td><td>Heathway
To</td></tr>
<tr><td>(8)
BANK or MOORGATE Via Mile End
or VICTORIA Via Temple
OR ANY INTERMEDIATE STATION
Bank&c</td><td>(8)

Bank&c</td></tr>
<tr><td>2/2 Z</td><td>FARE</td><td>2/2 Z</td></tr>
</table>

7399   7399

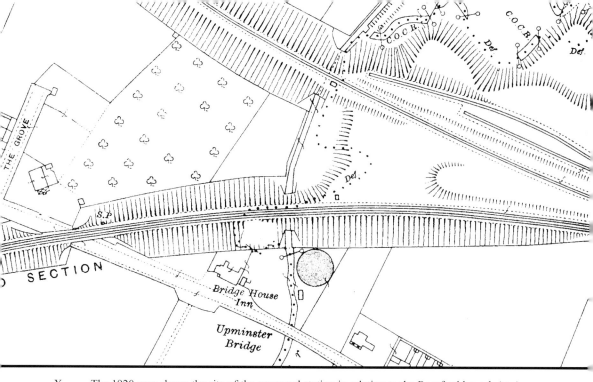

X. The 1920 map shows the site of the proposed station in relation to the Romford branch (top).

27. This eastward shot was taken from the end of the platform on 30th November 1957. This was before electrification and re-signalling and shows the Upminster West down distant signal. A substation for the District electric trains appears in the distance. A well known local landmark, the Upminster windmill, is visible on the skyline to the right. (F.Church)

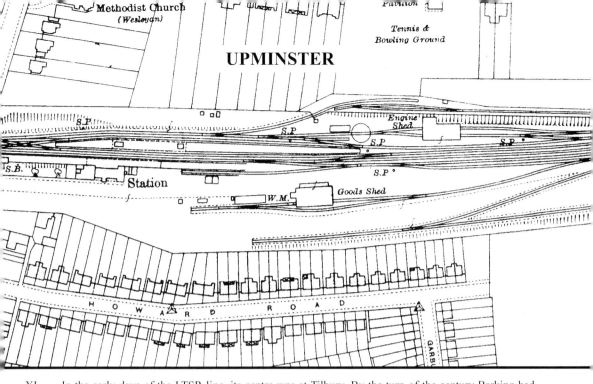

XI.   In the early days of the LTSR line, its centre was at Tilbury. By the turn of the century Barking had become a major junction and after 1908, was the largest station. However, many staff were employed in the Fenchurch Street offices and at Plaistow Works, while Southend and Upminster were also important centres. Upminster became a crossroad in 1893 when the route between Tilbury and Romford was completed. Having failed to keep the GER out of Southend, the LTS occupied the route which the GE might have taken to reach Tilbury Docks. Upminster was a crossroad site on this route, with the line to Romford going north, and that to West Thurrock Junction for Grays and Tilbury to the south. From 1932 Upminster became the end of the four track section from Barking and the terminal for the District line electric trains. This map is from 1920.

1. Early 20th Century

28.   Here we view the station masters house and the station buildings from the approach road. Initially Upminster had no more status than other wayside stations such as Laindon or Hornchurch and the buildings were similar. The private road led on to the goods yard, which closed on 7th December 1964. (G.W.Goslin)

29.   We now look from the overbridge at the London end of the station. It shows the arrangement after the opening of the Grays to Romford line in 1893. The down platform has been altered to an island platform and a small single road engine shed has been added on the down side. The short train probably came from Romford and will be leaving for Grays and Tilbury. (Commercial postcard)

→

30.   The next two photographs feature locomotives at Upminster before the transformation of 1932. The first was taken on Coronation Day, 22nd June 1911, and shows the 12.15pm from Fenchurch Street to Southend, which ran non-stop from Barking to Benfleet, but the photographer evidently decided to take it at Upminster. The late Kenneth Leech who was at Plaistow Works at the time, said that the elaborate decorations including the busts of the King and the Queen were rumoured to have cost £600. No. 80 *Thundersley* was built at Robert Stephenson's works in 1909. She was exhibited that year at the White City with a temporary change of name to *Southend-on-Sea*. On the day following the Coronation she worked an Orient Line boat train from St. Pancras to Tilbury, after which the decorations were removed. (K.Nunn/LCGB)

→

31.   The second shot shows a less distinguished locomotive no. 3 *Tilbury* built by Sharp, Stewart in 1880. She was adapted at Plaistow Works in 1902 with condensing gear and a new cab to work in the underground tunnel of the Whitechapel & Bow railway, jointly owned by the LTSR and the MDR. There is no record of her regularly working on this line but she was photographed on a goods train at Upminster in 1911. (K.Nunn/LCGB)

2. The 1920s

32.   Four photographs from 22nd August 1926 follow. The train bound for Fenchurch Street was hauled by no. 2149 built by Sharp, Stewart in 1897 and rebuilt in 1911 and 1920. 2149 was the Midland number of 1912; in 1929 she became LMS no. 2138 and in 1946 no. 1956; she was withdrawn in 1951. Her train consists of bogie compartment stock but on the far side of the island platform there is a rake of ex-LTSR 4-wheelers, probably in use on the Romford to Grays line. (H.C.Casserley)

33.   No. 2175 was built for the LTSR by the North British Locomotive Company in 1903 and survived until 1951. She displays her Southend via Upminster destination board but the LTSR sign and the route head code have been discontinued, although she does have lamps in a position to indicate an express train. This view includes the old station West Box, and such details as fire buckets, enamel advertisements, gas lamps and a porters trolley ready for handling the contents of guards vans. (H.C.Casserley)

34.   Two excursion trains were recorded. That from the Midland had its reporting number and was hauled by a somewhat venerable Johnson goods locomotive no. 3659. It must have been unusual for the crew to have placed lamps indicating an express train on a locomotive of this age and type. Let us hope that the excursionists, crammed into their Midland compartment stock had a prompt arrival and a good day at Southend. (H.C.Casserley)

35.   Those from the LNWR also had compartment coaches, but a more suitable locomotive, no. 1320 of the 'Prince of Wales' class. (H.C.Casserley)

3. Romford and Grays Services

This next group of Upminster pictures is devoted to trains on the Tilbury to Romford route. Particularly after the introduction of push-pull trains in 1934, an increasing proportion of the trains terminated in the bay platform at Grays. After Upminster became the terminal for the LT trains in 1932, the LT tracks separated the Romford and Tilbury sections of the cross country route. When the LT took over their tracks this separation was recognised. The Romford section was provided with a separate platform on the north side of the station and was operated as an Upminster branch of the LNER main line. When it was electrified it was only accessible from the north. Finally, instead of being operated as a cross country route, the line southwards was served by Fenchurch Street to Southend trains running via Upminster, Grays and Tilbury.

36.   This photograph was taken on 11th June 1938 and shows the 6.19pm about to depart for Tilbury. No. 1290 was one of the ex-Midland 0-4-4T locomotives fitted for working push-pull trains, which in 1934 replaced venerable LTS locomotives. The photograph was taken from the steps of the footbridge with empty coaching stock and the goods shed in the background. (H.C.Casserley)

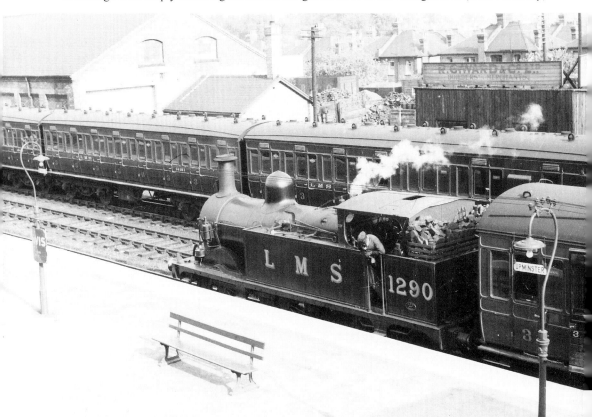

37.   This shot, taken on 20th August 1950, shows no. 58038 probably positioned for taking water. The ventilators of the engine shed plus the water tank may be seen over the top of the train. (E.Course)

38.   This panorama was taken from the footbridge on 24th March 1956. By this time the ex-MR 0-4-4T locomotives had been withdrawn and no. 41942 was heading the train running in from Grays. No. 41942 had been no. 2124, built for the LMS by Nasmyth Wilson in 1925 and withdrawn in 1956. (E.Course)

39.   To fill the gap until the diesel trains were available, the Eastern Region transferred locomotives from the former LNER. No. 69695 was of the N7 class built by Beardmore in 1927 and fitted for push-pull working in 1951. It was operating the Romford shuttle on 15th September 1956. Water is being taken in the traditional way with the driver controlling the water and the fireman perched on the tank. The brazier provides protection from freezing. (B.Pask)

40.   On 13th March 1957 no. 67363, an ex-Great Northern loco of LNER class C12 built at Doncaster Works in 1899, was on the Grays train. It is standing in the bay platform with the roof line of the original buildings visible above the train. (B.Pask)

41.   The line between West Thurrock Junction and Upminster was electrified as part of the LTS electrification and a view taken on 22nd May 1976 shows an electric train leaving Upminster for Grays. The lines on the left lead to the LT sidings; the water tank remains. (A.A.Jackson)

42.   Although the line between Upminster and West Thurrock Junction was electrified, the single line signalling remained unchanged. This photograph from 14th February 1976 shows the driver collecting the token for the Upminster to Ockendon section from the Upminster East Junction Signal Box. (A.A.Jackson)

44.   Taken after electrification the view of 20th April 1994 shows no. 315810 on the 14.56 departure for Romford. (M.Turvey)

43.   The Upminster to Romford section was separated from our route by the LT line and was given its separate platform (no. 6) in 1957. This is shown on 22nd May 1976 when the service was operated by diesel trains. The LT train alongside will make a much longer journey, across London, to terminate at Ealing Broadway. (A.A.Jackson)

45.   This photograph from 29th May 1990 looking towards Barking from the footbridge shows all three main platforms; the Romford platform is out of sight to the right and the original LTS buildings are on the left. (A.A.Jackson)

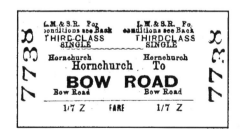

46.   Upminster shed was the base for the locomotives that worked on the Romford to Tilbury route. The original shed of 1893 was demolished in 1931 to make way for the District line trains. A new shed was provided in 1935. This had a single road. It was coded by the LMS as 13E and was, in effect, a sub shed or garage, for Plaistow, 13A. A picture from 11th June 1938 shows the second shed with its coaling stage and water tank. A Romford train headed by no. 1287 is in the foreground. (H.C.Casserley)

47.   By 24 March 1956, 13E had deteriorated and was finally closed in 1957. The N7 tank engine no. 69695 is visible with some coal wagons. Also to be seen was a Midland Railway platform seat and the extreme end of the RCTS special train run to celebrate the LTSR Centenary. (E.Course)

5. West of Upminster

48.   Two views were taken from the overbridge at the west end of the station looking along the wide cutting; in terms of extent, perhaps the heaviest earthwork on the route. This photograph must have been taken shortly before the opening of the electric tracks in 1932. The gentle slopes of the cutting sides indicate unstable subsoil; that on the left has a growth of shrubs but on the right, only grass has had time to establish itself. The down Southend train has a Tilbury tank locomotive running bunker first and the line for Romford has already been moved to the north side of the cutting. (LCGB)

49.   This photograph was taken on 19th July 1958 from the same place. The track layout and signal cabin appear little changed since 1932, but there are signs of overhead gantries for electrification. The Grays to Romford route was dieselised in 1958 and a Romford bound train is shown. (F.Church)

50.   This panorama from the end of the 20th century should be compared with pictures 48 and 49. The West Junction Signal Box has been demolished, and the gently sloping banks have more vegetation. The train from Fenchurch formed of Set No. 312725 is bound for Tilbury via Ockendon. The detached single line to Romford is visible on the right. (M.Turvey)

51.   Taken from the end of the station on 3rd April 2001, this shows one of the newly introduced units, no. 357014, leaving for Fenchurch Street. By the Autumn of 2001, most of the trains on the Southend direct line were formed of these units. (M.Turvey)

52.   This shows the new signalling centre, framed in the gantry supporting colour light signals. In 1994, the centre replaced the control system installed in the 1960s. The junction for the Ockendon line is just beyond the building and no. 312790 is about to turn on to the branch to Grays. (M.Turvey)

6. East of Upminster

53.　　Just over one mile to the east of Upminster was Cranham Signal Box and the brickworks siding, and in the vicinity was a spot favoured by the late Ken Nunn for photographic recording. On 5th August 1913 he photographed two contrasting trains. One was a through special excursion train from the North London line with a North London Railway 4-4-0T and coaches. According to Michael Robbins "On excursions to Southend hauled by NL engines some startling performances were achieved but no details have survived". Presumably the North London crew worked through with an LTS pilotman. To put it mildly, the passengers are unlikely to have reached Southend in comfort. (K.Nunn/LCGB)

54.   On the other hand he photographed the through train from Ealing via the District line, consisting of one of the two luxurious corridor trains introduced in 1912. Both the Tilbury and the Brighton companies normally carried all their passengers in compartment coaches, but the Brighton had provided alternative accommodation for some years. Although the LTS luxury trains had nearly as much time available between leaving the underground and reaching Southend as there was between Victoria and Brighton, there was never any on train catering (except on the Dunkirk boat trains). The locomotive no. 2107 was built by Beyer Peacock in 1912 and appears in Midland livery. These locomotives were banned from the viaduct leading to Fenchurch Street, but were able to take over from the District electric locomotives at Barking. (K.Nunn/LCGB)

55.   The Midland Railway was in charge from 1912 until 1923, but as this included four years of war, they did not have the opportunity to do a great deal. A minor activity was the erection of warning notices against trespass. One survived at Ockendon and another east of Upminster. In both cases the standard Midland wording, with a reference to powers included in the original Midland Act of 1844 (7 Vic. Cap. 18 Sec. 238) were used. The Upminster example photographed on 31st August 1958, bore the date **June 1906** which pre-dated the Midland takeover by 6 years. Presumably the casting was a product of Derby rather than Plaistow. (F.Church)

WEST HORNDON

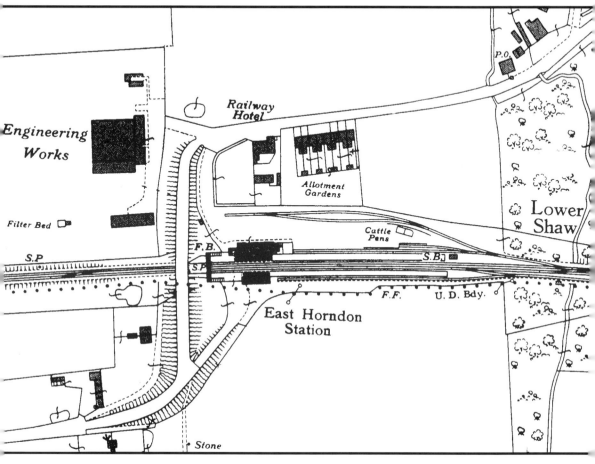

XII. East Horndon was opened on 1st May 1886 and was just under three miles east of Upminster. The choice of name was rather puzzling as the station was located in West Horndon and it is not surprising that when the Eastern Region took over in 1949, the station name was changed to West Horndon. Changes since 1886 have been mainly negative. The signal box was closed in 1961 and the goods depot on 7th September 1964. The shelter on the down side was removed, but the LTSR buildings on the up side survived in 2001. The map is from 1940.

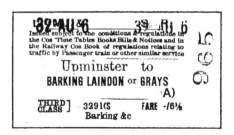

56.   These two photographs were taken on 27th October 1957. The first shows the station mainly as opened with the beginnings of a modest station garden on the left. Level crossings were avoided on the direct line so ramps were constructed leading to overbridges. East Horndon had the usual wayside station arrangement with the station approach road forking off short of the ramp. In 1957 there were still coal wagons in the yard. (F.Church)

57.   No. 90449 was one of the WD 2-10-0s and is seen shunting wagons carrying girders for a bridge replacement over the Tilbury to Brentwood road. We can also see the original signal box. The setting was rural until after World War II when Brown & Tawse moved onto a greenfield site which had a private siding for their steel traffic. In 2000 a railway stores depot, long established between Gidea Park and Romford, was moved to West Horndon; it had no siding. (F.Church)

EAST OF WEST HORNDON

58.   Increasing traffic on the direct line led to the opening of three new signal boxes to break up the longer block sections between Barking and Pitsea; Gale Street in 1906, Dunton in 1905 and Basildon in 1898. (The section between Dagenham and Hornchurch was covered by the River Rom intermediate signals of 1912, operated automatically by track circuits). Dunton Signal Box, photographed on 5th June 1910, broke up the three and a half miles beween East Horndon and Laindon. The lower part of the post of the down home signal is visible at the top of the bank on the right; the picture was probably taken from the up home post. The timber box is of the standard type built by the Railway Signal Co. for the LTS. The signalman posed himself carrying out his duty of checking the down train. This was recorded as a Chalk Farm to Southend through train passed, hauled by no. 31 *St. Pancras* which was built by Nasmyth Wilson in 1892. It is noteworthy that at this time the tops of sleepers were left uncovered by ballast at regular intervals. (K.Nunn/LCGB)

59.   In 1925 the LMS replaced Dunton by two signal boxes Dunton East and Dunton West, both of a Midland design. The view of 14th December 1957 shows Dunton East which, like its predecessor operated signals only. It is interesting that the return to manual operation probably planned in the Midland period, was a reversion from the automatic electrical working introduced by the LTS in 1912. The photograph includes the lamp room and a convenience for the signal man. The down train of LMS coaches is hauled by no. 42634, a standard 2-6-4T built at Derby in 1934. (F.Church)

LAINDON

XIII. The station opened on 1st June 1888, and was built to serve a predominantly rural area, although there was a very modest excursion traffic to the nearby Langdon Hills. However cheap land attracted developers who created an odd landscape of unmetalled roads bordering squares bearing scattered informal buildings. After WWII, Laindon developed in a more conventional way, alongside the new town of Basildon. This is the 1939 survey.

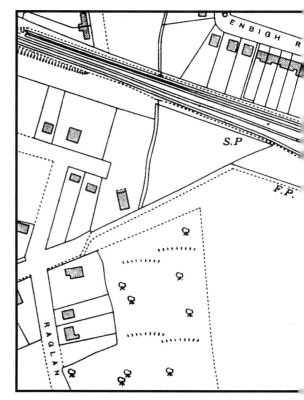

60. The first view shows the station virtually as opened in 1888. The typical LTS buildings including the station masters house appear on the left, with the goods yard, destined for closure on 5th June 1967, beyond. (Commercial postcard)

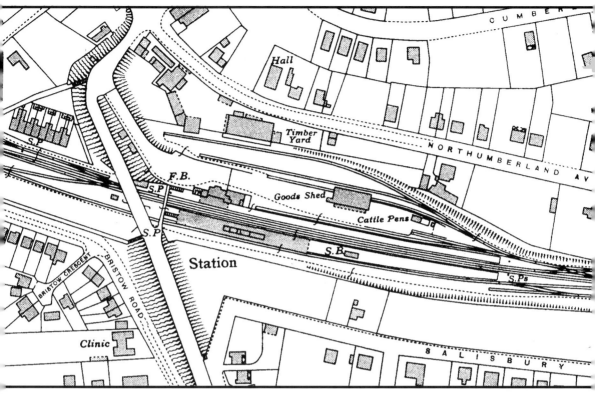

61.   In 1933, to allow for trains waiting at Laindon, the up platform was made into an island, a third line providing a passing loop for up trains. In 1957 the passing loop became the up main and the former up main became reversible. In this view from 6th September 1958, evidence of development includes a personal weighing machine and a Finlays Tobacco Kiosk. There has been some adaption of the original LTS buildings; at one time they were in use as an estate agents office. (F.Church)

BASILDON

62.   During the electrification period Bridge 85 was replaced to accommodate the road network of the emergent new town of Basildon. No. 42502, one of the 3 cylinder batch of 1934, is shown crossing a temporary bridge on 8th February 1958. (F.Church)

63.   The new station of Basildon was not opened until 25th November 1974. It had buildings down at ground level and needless to say, no freight facilities. It was photographed on 3rd April 2001, with a Fenchurch Street train consisting of Set No. 357014 leading and 357023 trailing, leaving the station. (M.Turvey)

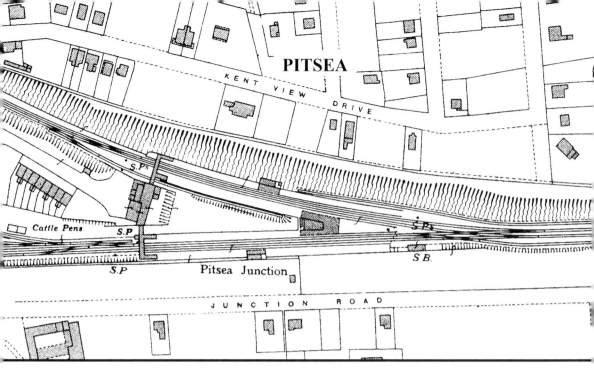

XIV.   Pitsea was opened in 1855 on the extension from Tilbury to Southend. When the direct line of 1888 was designed, Pitsea was selected as the site for its junction with the original line. New buildings were erected in the fork between the two routes with platforms on both lines, short of the junction. However, the existing goods depot on the Tilbury side remained in use and is shown on the 1939 edition.

64.   The original line to Tilbury is on the left and the direct line to Barking via Upminster curves away to the right. (Commercial postcard)

65.   We now have a similar perspective from a train approaching the junction on 21st June 1986. The panel signal box of 1960 is sited on the converging platforms. (A.A.Jackson)

66.   We look towards the junction with the direct line on the left. It shows how the restricted site necessitated the provision of the massive retaining wall with blind arches. The LTS station buildings and station masters house are on the right. The tall signal post, with co-acting arms, was necessitated by a degree of visual obstruction by the bridge from which the photograph was taken. (Commercial postcard)

67.   The 16th February 1958 was the date of this view from the Tilbury platform showing in essence the second Pitsea of 1888. Only the concrete lampposts are new. (F.Church)

68.   The photograph taken on 8th June 1958 shows the direct line platforms, a new concrete footbridge in addition to the 1888 bridge and the signal box of 1934, which is largely obscured by the canopy. (F.Church)

70.   This view from 3rd April 2001 shows no. 312798 entering Pitsea on a down train. The severity of the curve is reflected by the instruction on the edge of the platform to "Mind the Gap". (M.Turvey)

69.   The next two pictures feature the massive retaining wall which, apart from the bridges and one viaduct, is the most impressive engineering work on the LTS. Seen on 23rd June 1957 is no. 44442, built at Crewe in 1927 to the Midland design, on a down Southend excursion. Having coasted down from Laindon and reduced speed for the Pitsea curve, the locomotive was blowing off steam and doubtless the fireman was relaxing. (F.Church)

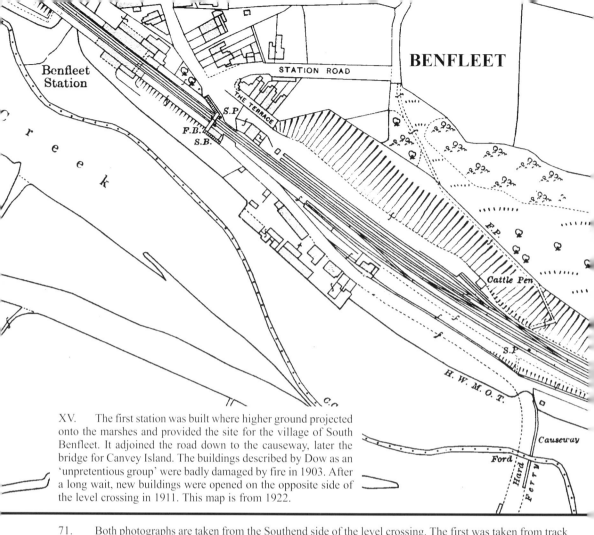

BENFLEET

Benfleet
Station

STATION ROAD

THE TERRACE

S.P.

F.B.

S.B.

Cattle Pen

Creek

F.P.

S.P.

H. W. M. O. T.

Causeway

Ford

Hard

Ferry

XV.   The first station was built where higher ground projected onto the marshes and provided the site for the village of South Benfleet. It adjoined the road down to the causeway, later the bridge for Canvey Island. The buildings described by Dow as an 'unpretentious group' were badly damaged by fire in 1903. After a long wait, new buildings were opened on the opposite side of the level crossing in 1911. This map is from 1922.

71.   Both photographs are taken from the Southend side of the level crossing. The first was taken from track level on 22nd July 1958 with BR standard 2-6-4T no. 42254 leaving with a train for Southend. The signal box was opened with the new station in 1911. It finished as a block post in 1964, but continued to operate the level crossing until that was closed in 1977. The end of a group of railway cottages appears on the right. (F.Church)

72.   The second view, taken from an up train on 21st June 1986, shows the buildings of 1911 virtually unaltered. The platforms were built above ground level and incorporated a crossing over a creek; they were linked by a subway. The main buildings were in a pleasant traditional style and incorporated the station masters house. Particularly since WWII the population of Benfleet and of Canvey Island has increased greatly, leading to a substantial growth of traffic at the station. (A.A.Jackson)

WEST OF LEIGH-ON-SEA

73.   Considerable lengths of the LTS were built across marshland in a straight line, without earthworks, and the line between Benfleet and Leigh-on-Sea was typical. After the descent beyond Benfleet there were nearly four miles of straight, level track with no earthworks. This is illustrated by a view taken from the new Leigh-on-Sea Station in evening light with a train on its way back to St. Pancras. (B.Pask)

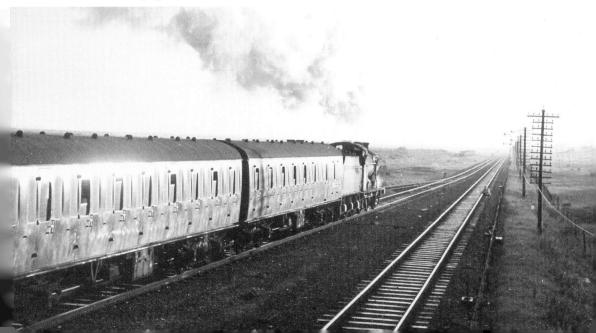

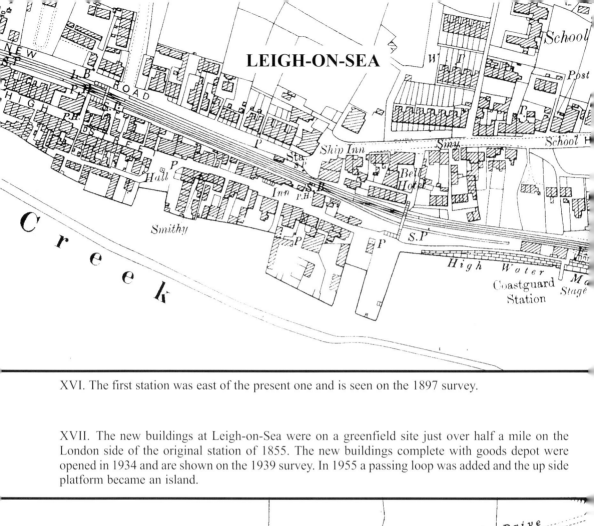

XVI. The first station was east of the present one and is seen on the 1897 survey.

XVII. The new buildings at Leigh-on-Sea were on a greenfield site just over half a mile on the London side of the original station of 1855. The new buildings complete with goods depot were opened in 1934 and are shown on the 1939 survey. In 1955 a passing loop was added and the up side platform became an island.

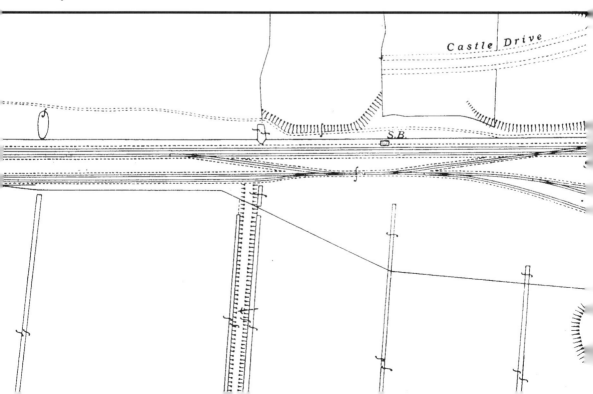

74.   The route suffered badly in the floods of 1953, particularly on the sections traversing marshland near Tilbury and near Southend. The first of the flood photographs was taken on 1st February 1953 by which time the platforms were above the level of the water. It shows the up home signal and the flooded goods yard. (J.Mann/LCGB)

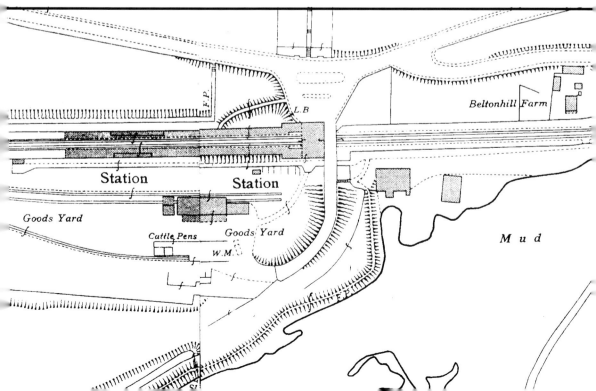

75.   This shows the signal box on the same date. The fishing village of Leigh was located where higher ground came down to the water. Originally the LTS was planned to divert inland through a cutting avoiding the village, but its powers were amended to permit it to squeeze along the backs of the houses on the High Street. The railway cut off the village from its waterfront and wharf, so a level crossing was provided to preserve access. A station was fitted in on the London side of this level crossing. Facilities were slightly improved in 1896 when a new up platform was opened on the opposite side of the crossing. This arrangement, with staggered platforms, lasted until 1934 when the new station was opened. (J.Mann/LCGB)

76.   This photograph was taken on 22nd December 1957 looking towards Southend. No. 42524, one of the original 3 cylinder 2-6-4T locomotives built for the Tilbury line, runs round a train which was standing on the centre road. The residences in the background occupy the higher ground above the old fishing village. (E.Course)

77.   A photograph of 25th July 1958 was taken from the disused down platform of 1855, looking towards Southend. It shows the signal box and the up platform of 1896. An up train was approaching, hauled by no. 80136, a standard BR 2-6-4T locomotive. (F.Church)

78.   This picture dated 2nd December 1957 was taken from the footbridge at the level crossing looking towards London. (The old village was on the left and post railway housing, along New Road, on the right). Also on the right are some remains of the old down platform. The signal post carries four arms, two home and two distant, to give improved visibility. Drainage works were in progress. (F.Church)

79.   The new station of 1934 is shown in this photograph from 21st October 1989 looking towards Southend. The platforms were built down on the marsh, but the buildings were placed across the platforms on a new road which descended from the higher ground. The up platform which appears on the right, became an island when the passing loop was added. (A.A.Jackson)

EAST OF LEIGH-ON-SEA

80.   The next mile of the line will be carried in the memories of all those East End children whose first seaside outing was to Southend. After miles of unremarkable countryside followed by marshland, they would have their first sight of the sea, if the tide was in. The line ran between the higher ground and the top of the beach - the LTS equivalent of Dawlish. (Commercial poscard)

81.   This photograph shows two rarities - an LTSR goods train bound for Southend and an LTSR trespass notice. Until the 0-6-2T locomotives became available, goods trains were hauled by the same engines as the passenger trains. This is no. 11 *Stratford* of the No. 1 class built by Sharp Stewart in 1880. (LCGB)

CHALKWELL

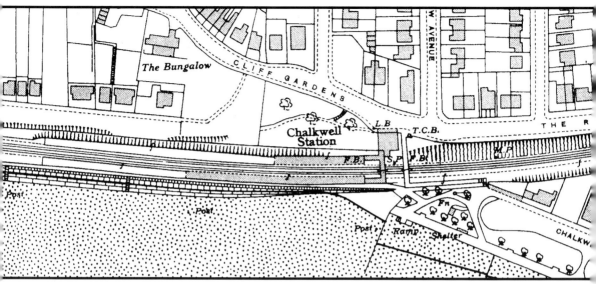

XVIII. The original plan was to follow the top of the beach to a terminal adjoining the pier. Not surprisingly, this aroused great opposition and another alignment was substituted rather more than quarter of a mile inland. This necessitated a climb at 1 in 94 from the shoreline, initially on an embankment and then in a cutting. Chalkwell was opened on 11th September 1933 at the point at which the line turned inland to commence the climb to Westcliff and is shown on the 1939 edition.

82.   The view of 21st October 1989 shows the station as seen from a down train. The station handled passenger traffic only, with two side platforms and buildings up at road level. (A.A.Jackson)

83.   This photograph was taken from the Crowstone Road footbridge on 10th November 1958 and shows a train climbing the gradient up from Chalkwell to Westcliff, drawn by no. 2505. The photograph also shows a ramp for the Hudd automatic warning system and the overground telegraph line. (F.Church)

XIX. This was always a high class area. The station was requested by developers including members of the Brassey family, who provided the land plus £1500 towards the construction costs. The best express trains all called, although the LTS maintained the 50 minute schedule from Southend to Fenchurch Street. The name Kensington-on-Sea was considered but Westcliff was the final choice. This is the 1939 edition and shows the proximity of the low cliffs to the station.

84. This is the view from Hamlet Court Road Bridge with the station virtually as opened in 1895. The prestigious buildings are on the up platform; an LTS train is running in on the down side. (Commercial Postcard)

85. This is no. 30 *Fenchurch* of the No. 1 class built by Sharp Stewart in 1884 which survived until 1934. The down train consists of a mixture of LTS coaches. The houses in the background were built in Britannia Road - a name with a period flavour - while the houses reflect the class of person travelling from Westcliff. There was a world of difference between the East End terraces from which the passengers on the train had come and the comfortable residences, with maid servants in which Westcliff commuters lived. (LCGB)

86. This record from the up platform was made on 23rd August 1955 with a train leaving for London. It shows a traditional scene with lineside allotments for railwaymen.
(H.C.Casserley)

87. The RCTS Southend Centenary Special of 11th March 1956 ran down the original route via Stratford, Barking and Tilbury. The locomotive was the last surviving passenger engine of the LTSR (BR no. 41966) and was built by Robert Stephenson in 1909. This was restored to LTS livery for the centenary with the original name *Thundersley*. Subsequently it was placed on exhibition at Bressingham. The leading coach, LTS no. 283, was also restored but unfortunately later destroyed. Some of the details, including the position of the names on the destination board, are not quite correct. (P.Hay)

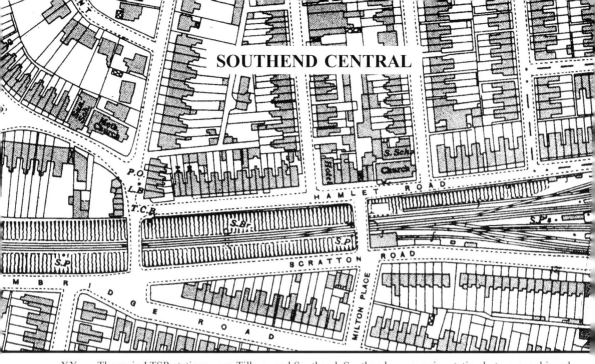

SOUTHEND CENTRAL

XX. The main LTSR stations were Tilbury and Southend. Southend was a major station but never achieved the status of Brighton. Whereas Southend was as popular as Brighton for London day trippers, it did not do as well for longer visits; it had only one grand hotel. Moreover, at Brighton nearly all the season ticket holders used the main station, but at Southend they were distributed amongst the various stations, and some used the GE route. Nevertheless it was a main station reaching its greatest importance from the 1900s to the 1950s, apart from the war periods. It was the station known and remembered by thousands of East End day trippers most of whom would have used it bcause they would not know of any other stations. The original buildings were replaced in 1889, in response to the GER "invasion" and basically these were the buildings in use in 2001. Platform accommodation was increased by providing bays on the outside of the main platforms. They are shown in 1939.

88. The final platform extension was completed in 1899 as shown. It consisted of the addition of an extra island platform (nos. 5 and 6), as shown on the right. More sidings were added for empty trains. The signal box at the end of the widened platform 3/4 remained until 1960. The goods shed of 1881, enlarged in 1929, appears on the left near to the chimney of the brewery. (Commercial postcard)

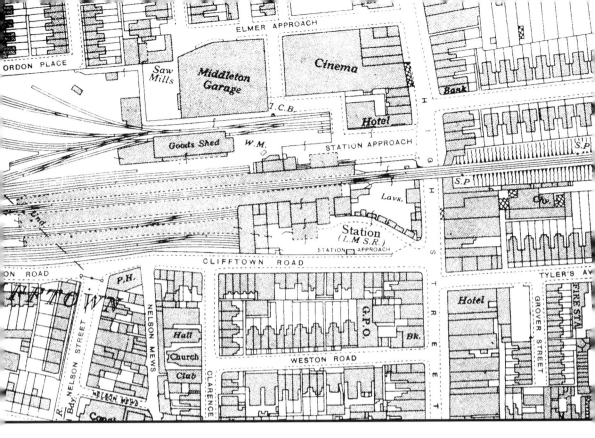

89.　　The site of the station was at the end of a cutting and this view, dated 3rd August 1958, was taken from the overbridge at the London end of the station. It shows a return excursion from the former LNWR line backing into platform 5. The locomotive was no. 42870, a 'Crab' Mogul built at Crewe in 1930 and withdrawn in 1963. Although this was the twilight of the day excursion, other trains are visible on the sidings. (F.Church)

90.   This photograph was taken from the bank at the London end of the station on 18th April 1960. Electrification work was underway and a new panel signal box was being constructed on the left. The train was leaving from platform 2 and for identification appears to have 'T12' and 'Tilbury' chalked on the smokebox door. The locomotive is standard BR 2-6-4T no. 80075. (B.Pask)

91.   This shot from 21st October 1989 was taken from a down train approaching the station. Electrification and resignalling had been completed over 20 years earlier and with the virtual end of excursion traffic, platforms 5 and 6 had been removed. The goods depot had been closed, with the end of goods traffic in the Southend area on 5th June 1967. (A.A.Jackson)

92.   The scene on 22nd September 1990 was recorded from the widened platform 3/4. It shows a down EMU train approaching and the panel signal box of 1960. Somewhat unusually, it also shows another photographer. (A.A.Jackson)

93.   The main entrance in 2000 showed only detailed changes since its completion in 1889. The first station was opened as 'Southend' in 1856 and became 'Southend-on-Sea' in 1876, 'Southend-on-Sea Central' in 1949 and, significantly, 'Southend Central' in 1969. It is situated inconspicuously in a side road off the High Street. The new company name, 'c2c', appears on the canopy. There is no memorial to the thousands of day trippers who would have used this entrance for their day by the sea. (E.Course)

SOUTHEND EAST

XXI. The site of the original terminus became hemmed in. The extension to Shoeburyness in 1884 enabled the locomotive depot plus some carriage sidings to be moved there. However, in 1908 more carriage and goods sidings were constructed about half a mile along the Shoeburyness extension and were known as 'Southend Sidings'. Passenger facilities at Southend East were not provided until 1932 and additional accommodation for trains was completed at that time. The up platform was reconstructed as an island and a new side platform was added one year later. This is the 1939 map.

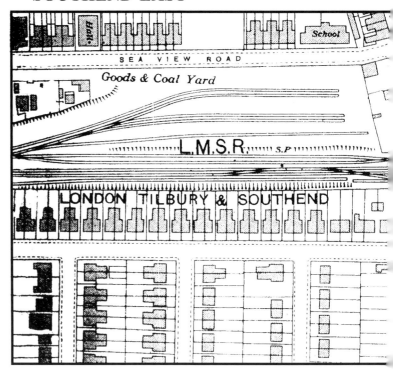

94.   The main part of the sidings was at ground level and as the running lines were descending into a cutting, the junction for the sidings was nearer to Southend. A trackside view on 3rd August 1958 shows the Southend Sidings signal box adjoining the junction. The approaching up train was hauled by no. 42520, one of the original 2-6-4T locomotives built for the Tilbury line in 1934. (F.Church)

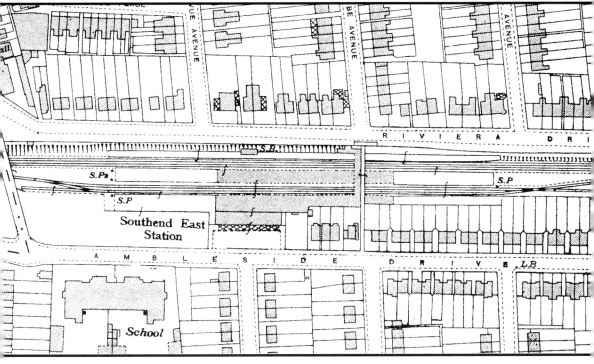

95.   Looking from Southchurch Avenue bridge on 4th May 1958 towards Shoeburyness, Southend Sidings appear on the left. They were closed in 1967 and the site was later occupied by housing development. The railway connection was recognised in the road names - Fowler Close, Stanier Close and Fairburn Close. They contain wagons for liquid and for solid fuels and also passenger coaches. Other sidings were placed on each side of the running lines for empty trains. BR no. 80101 is approaching on a Tilbury train. (F.Church)

96.   From the Chase Road overbridge on 4th June 1958, looking to Shoeburyness, it was possible to see all the platforms and the signal box. The up train was hauled by no. 42678, a 2 cylinder 2-6-4T locomotive built for the LMS. With the end of the day excursions and of freight traffic, there was no need for all the platforms or for the sidings. The goods sidings were closed on 5th June 1967 and the extra passenger platform in 1982. The two platforms on the running lines remained in use, but the side platform and impressive entrance which adjoined it in Ambleside Drive were abandoned. The entrance on the opposite side, in Riviera Drive, was upgraded to handle the remaining passenger traffic. (F.Church)

97.   The site of the abandoned platform had not been sold as shown in this photograph of 29th November 2001 and the up side entrance remained out of use. (E.Course)

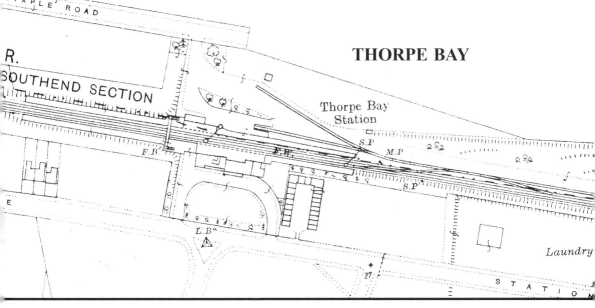

Thorpe Bay
Station

XXII. Whereas Westcliff was opened by the LTSR only three quarters of a mile to the west of Southend, Thorpe Bay was two and a quarter miles to the east. In both cases the developers provided the land but Thorpe Bay did not develop in the same way as Westcliff. When it was opened on 1st July 1910, it was called after the neighbouring village, Southchurch, but after only 18 days it took its name from Colonel Burges's Thorpe Hall Estate. The buildings were well up to Westcliff standards. The booking office and station masters house formed an attractive block, facing onto a semi-circular station approach, which enclosed a garden. This map is from 1922.

98.   An early photograph taken from the down platform records the station as built. (G.W.Goslin coll.)

99.   A photograph of 4th May 1911 shows the up through train to Ealing via the District line, before special coaches were provided. The locomotive was LTSR no. 46 *Southchurch* of the 37 class, built by Dubs & Co. in 1898 and withdrawn in 1951. The signal box which adjoined the points for the goods yard is visible beyond the rear of the train. (K.Nunn/LCGB)

————————▶

100.   The road side of the buildings was photographed on 25th October 1961 and externally shows virtually no change since 1910. However, the booking hall was refurbished by c2c and fitted with automatic ticket barriers. (B.Pask)

————————▶

101.   A shot from the same position as used for picture 98, taken on a gloomy 29th November 2001, shows how little had changed. Electrification necessitated the erection of the gantries and the new footbridge; electric lights had replaced the gas lamps and the platform had been resurfaced. (E.Course)

SHOEBURYNESS

XXIII. The extension from Southend to Shoeburyness in 1884 was built to serve the military establishment. To give easy access to all platforms, buildings at terminals were often erected across the ends of the tracks, but at Shoeburyness they were at the side. Unusually for the LTSR they consisted of a single storey building of timber, with no station masters house. The engine shed was moved here from Southend and sidings were provided for the storage of carriages. With electrification and the use of EMUs the carriage sidings were extended. Curving across this 1939 survey are military lines, which are detailed in the next map.

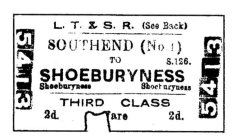

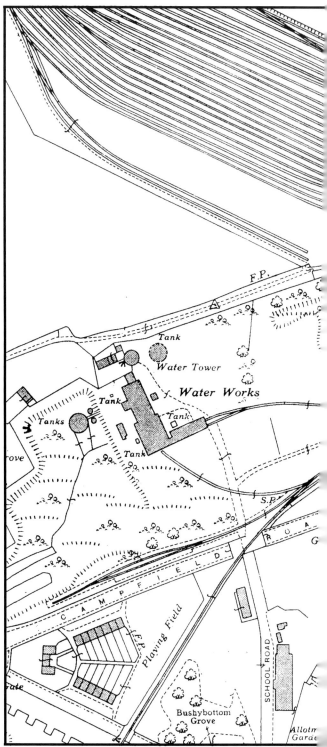

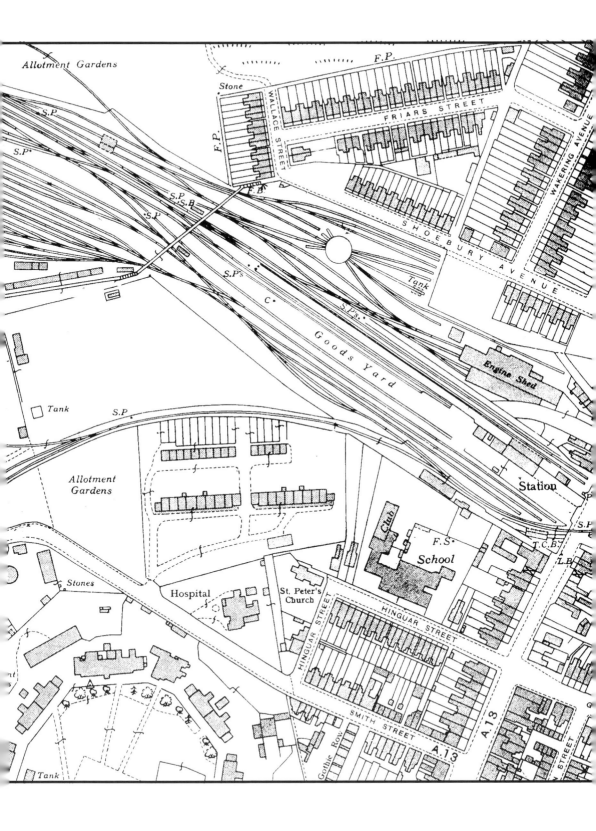

Allotment Gardens

S.P

S.P

S.P.
S.P.
S.P
S.P

Stone

F.P.
F.P.

WALLACE STREET

F.P.

FRIARS STREET

F.P.

SHOEBURY AVENUE

WAKERING AVENUE

S.P's.

C

Tank

S.Ps.

Goods Yard

Tank

S.P.

Allotment
Gardens

Engine Shed

Station

S.P.

S.P.

Club

F.S.

School

T.C.B.

L.B.

Stones

Hospital

St. Peter's
Church

HINGUAR STREET

HINGUAR STREET

SMITH STREET

GOTHIC ROW

A.13

A.13

STREET

Tank

102. The carriage sidings were well filled on 4th May 1958. Near the water crane is 2-6-4T no. 42530. (F.Church)

103. A prone photographer takes a shot on 11th March 1956 of the restored LTS coach no. 283 built by Cravens in 1910. It was the leading coach on the RCTS Centenary Special, being restored for the occasion but later destroyed. Photograph no. 87 shows the train standing at Westcliff. (E.Course)

104.   On 28th December 1960 a steam train was leaving from the main platform no. 2. The locomotive is a standard BR 2-6-4T and the coach is from the LNER. The goods yard closed on 5th June 1967. (R.F.Orpwood/Gresley Society)

105.   The scene on 25th April 1970 included the two main platforms with a train in the bay platform. (First class compartments indicated by numerals on the doors). The wooden buildings with a platform canopy are visible in the middle distance. (A.A.Jackson)

106. The rubbish at the end of the 'Misery Line' justified the name on 17th January 1981. Fortunately the management has improved recently. The last of the class 310 units operated on 18th November 2001. (B.Morrison)

107. A special occasion was on the 28th August 2000, when the 'Cockney Coaster' arrived in platform 1. The locomotive was numbered 45157 and named *Glasgow Highlander*. However its original number was 45407. The train consisted of nine Mark 1 BR coaches, and during the day made two round trips between Fenchurch Street and Shoeburyness. (E.Course)

Locomotive Shed

108.   Excursion trains brought a variety of locomotives to Shoeburyness for servicing, in preparation for their return trips. No. 25602 *Bonadventure* of the LNWR 'Prince of Wales' class arrived from an excursion on 27th June 1936. (H.F.Wheeller/R.S.Carpenter)

109.   Apart from the sub shed at Upminster, Shoeburyness was the only locomotive depot between Barking and Southend on the direct line. A photograph taken in LTS days shows the original two road shed of 1884 with a lean-to added at the side. The water tank appears on the left and a water crane between the tracks. The locomotives are no. 11 *Stratford* built by Sharp Stewart in 1880 and no. 63 *Mansion House* delivered by the North British Locomotive Company in 1903. (LCGB)

110.   A view from 25th October 1961 shows how little the shed altered over the years. The only noteworthy change is that the lean-to was rebuilt with two roads in the 1950s. However, it has lost part of its roof. The locomotives, all 2-6-4T engines are, from left to right, nos. 42519, 42681 and 42684. (B.Pask)

111.   Shoeburyness was the only engine shed on the former Tilbury system to have a ferro-concrete mechanical coaling plant. It had a capacity of 100 tons which could be discharged into the bunkers or tenders of the locomotives through any one of the three chutes. It was commissioned in 1933, but the photograph was taken on 7th August 1960. The locomotive coal wagons, which were hoisted and tipped, appear on the left. The locomotive is no. 43964, an ex-MR class 4F 0-6-0 with a 14B (Kentish Town) shed plate on the smokebox door. The fireman is shown descending the ramp from the controls wearing a knotted white handkerchief on his head, and probably cycle clips as favoured by young firemen at the time. The engine shed was closed in 1962. (F.Church)

East of Shoeburyness

112.　　Named because its destination was the Shoeburyness MOD Depot on the Pig's Bay, Hertfordshire Railtours 'Prize Porker' railtour ran on 18th March 1995 from Paddington and returned to London Victoria. Traversing the short branch line from the station to the depot, and providing the unique sight of a passenger train on the line, RES no. 47737 *Resourceful* nears journey's end as it passes through the East Beach Caravan Park. (B.Morrison)

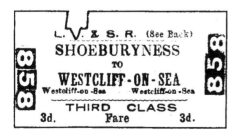

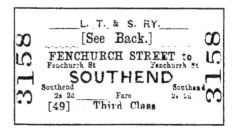

Ministry of Defence

XXIV. The Board of Ordnance purchased land at Shoeburyness for gun testing in 1849 and the School of Gunnery, with barracks, was opened in 1863. Communication was mainly by water, particularly with Woolwich Arsenal. A military railway linked different parts of the establishment with the piers and this was adapted to connect with the LTSR in 1884. The original line to the south of the LTS remained, but a more extensive system with numerous branches and sidings, was constructed to the north passing beyond Pig's Bay to Haven Point and New England Creek, about 5¼ miles from the southern extremity. In 1953, when it was fully operational it had about 20 steam and diesel standard gauge locomotives. BR ended freight service to the site in 1992, after which the southern section of the military railway was abandoned and the northern section little used. However, this was later found to be a very suitable place for storing main line coaches. The diagram is from 1959. (Railway Magazine)

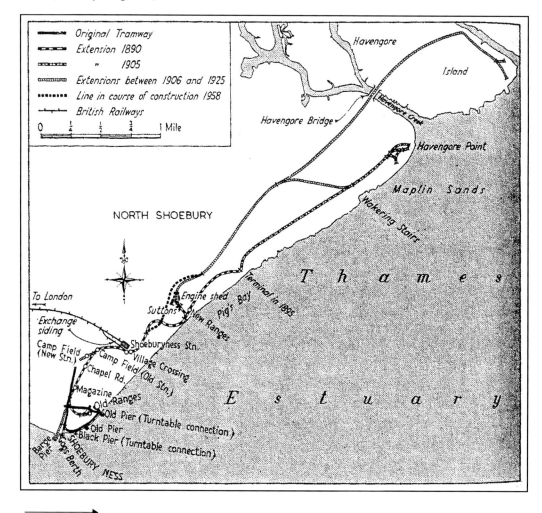

XXV. The 1939 survey has been reduced to about 17ins to 1 mile to show the southern part of the system and the 'Engine Houses'.

113.   The line had a fleet of Hunslet 0-6-0 STs. The location is Suttons Yard and the year is 1965.
(Major (Retd) A.Hill, MoD, Shoeburyness)

114.   The passenger rolling stock consisted largely of secondhand vehicles from a number of
companies. In use on 23rd August 1955 were ex-Cambrian and Great Eastern coaches. (E.Course)

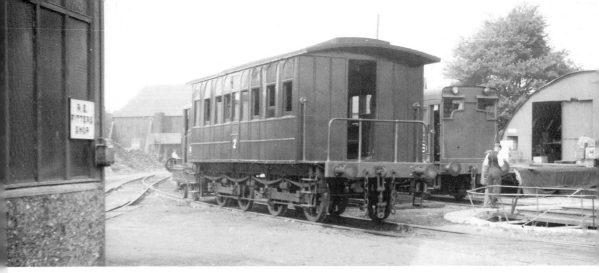

115.   Perhaps the most exotic coach was no. 3/2189 an 8-wheel rigid wheelbase saloon with open end platforms. It carried a brass plate inscribed "This coach did service on the Suakim-Berber Railway. It is reported to have been the saloon coach used by Lord Kitchener". It was returned from the Sudan and used at Shoeburyness for carrying VIPs including King George V. The picture also shows parts of two of the diesel locomotives, the turntable and the Royal Engineers Fitters Shop. (E.Course)

116.   With little military use, several miles of track and military security, the Shoeburyness railway had obvious advantages for the storage of superfluous main line coaching stock. The 'Railway Magazine' of September 2001 reported that 400 railway vehicles were stored on it and reproduced this aerial photograph showing the Pig's Bay area. Most of the rolling stock consists of withdrawn EMUs and DMUs currently off Railtrack registration. In effect, the Shoeburyness Military Railway has become a railway coach park. (M.Page)

SOUTHEND PIER RAILWAY

This began with a horse worked line that ran along the pier to connect with steamers, but was closed in 1881. Nine years later a new electric railway was opened, perhaps inspired by the Volks Electric Railway of 1883. Initially it was single line, but later passing loops were added. It was rebuilt in 1930 with double track and a signalling system. The coaches were replaced in 1949 and the peak year when the line carried four million passengers was 1950. After that, with the decline of day excursion traffic, receipts fell and finally the railway closed at the end of the season in 1978. It was reopened in 1986 as a single track line with diesel traction.

117.   In 1930 the route of one and a quarter miles was relaid with 3ft 6ins gauge double track with the live rail in the centre. Two signal boxes, each controlling crossovers, were installed about 200 yards outside each of the terminals. This photograph was taken on 25th April 1970 from the Shore End signal box during the winter season. It shows one of the seven car sets, supplied by AC Cars Ltd in 1949. Being the winter season only one track and one train would have been in use. (A.A.Jackson)

118.   The interior of the box was recorded on the same day, when it was out of use as the Summer season had not started. Of the seven levers two operated the crossing points, four operated the home and starter signals for the no. 1 and no. 2 tracks and one was for switching out the box. The signals consisted of colour lights showing two aspects. (A.A.Jackson)

3	4	5	6	7
POINTS CROSSOVER & BARS	POINTS CROSSOVER & BARS	SIGNAL FROM SHORE Nº2-Nº1 LINE 4 or 7	SIGNAL FROM SHORE ON Nº1 LINE	SWITCH OUT LEVER WITH KEY B

119.   The Shore End and Pier Head stations each consisted of wooden island platforms, roofed over. This picture shows one of the 1949 trains on 25th April 1970 at Shore End, presumably out of use in the winter season. The smaller of the two signs bears the warning "Danger, Electric Railway". (A.A.Jackson)

120.   The last view is from 26th July 1986 and was taken from the end of the platform at the Pier Head station. It shows the diesel train obtained that year, running in off the single track. (A.A.Jackson)

Also from Middleton Press is *Southend-on-Sea Tramways* which includes further views of the Southend Pier Railway. A special feature shows trams running on sleepered tracks through wooded areas east of the town and also the unusual coal tram.

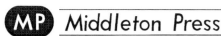

Middleton Press

Easebourne Lane, Midhurst
West Sussex. GU29 9AZ

A-0 906520 B-1 873793 C-1 901706 D-1 904474

OOP Out of Print at time of printing - Please check current availability **BROCHURE AVAILABLE SHOWING NEW TITLES**
Tel:01730 813169   www.middletonpress.com   email:info@middletonpress.co.uk